A LAND OF
Big Dreamers

VOICES OF COURAGE IN AMERICA

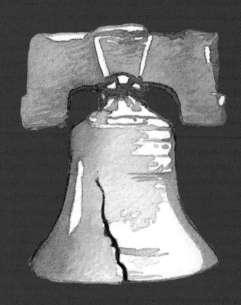

NEIL WALDMAN

MILLBROOK PRESS
MINNEAPOLIS

THE PAGES OF THIS BOOK FEATURE THE WORDS OF THIRTEEN GREAT AMERICANS.

These men and women distinguished themselves by acting courageously, often in difficult times, leaving a profound imprint on the history of our nation. As Senator Robert F. Kennedy wrote: *"It is from the numberless diverse acts of courage and belief that human history is shaped. Each time a man stands up for an ideal, or acts to improve the lot of others, he sends forth a tiny ripple of hope."*

FOR ROBERT CASILLA, CORNELIUS VAN WRIGHT, KALIMAH SAMIULLAH, AND CHRISSY PAPPAS, THE DEDICATED TEACHERS OF THE FRED DOLAN ART ACADEMY

Millbrook Press
A division of Lerner Publishing Group, Inc.
241 First Avenue North
Minneapolis, MN 55401 U.S.A.

Website address: www.lernerbooks.com

Excerpt on page 22 was reprinted by arrangement with The Heirs to the Estate of Martin Luther King Jr., c/o Writers House as agent for the proprietor New York, NY. *Copyright 1963 Dr. Martin Luther King Jr; copyright renewed 1991 Coretta Scott King*

Library of Congress Cataloging-in-Publication Data

A land of big dreamers : voices of courage in America / selected and illustrated by Neil Waldman.
  p.   cm.
ISBN: 978-0-8225-6810-0 (lib. bdg. : alk. paper)
  1. United States—History—Anecdotes—Juvenile literature. 2. United States—Biography—Anecdotes—Juvenile literature. 3. Courage—United States—Anecdotes—Juvenile literature. 4. National characteristics, American—Anecdotes—Juvenile literature. I. Waldman, Neil.
E178.6.L34 2011
973—dc22   2010001185

Manufactured in the United States of America
1 – VI – 12/31/10

CONTENTS

1776

THOMAS JEFFERSON

We hold these truths to be self-evident,
that all men are created equal . . .

These are the opening words of the U.S. Declaration of Independence. Written by Thomas Jefferson, the declaration was adopted by members of the Continental Congress on July 4, 1776, in Philadelphia, Pennsylvania. It explained why the people in America no longer wanted to be ruled by Great Britain. They were taking the courageous step of breaking away and forming a new nation.

The Declaration of Independence marked a turning point in the American Revolution (1775–1783) that pitted the underdog Americans against the British troops. After years of fighting, the Americans won. The dream of a new nation, the United States of America, became reality.

ELIZABETH CADY STANTON

We hold these truths to be self-evident:

that all men and women are created equal . . .

Not every American was granted equal rights in 1776. Although several states allowed women to vote (against the advice of the federal government), most states did not. In the 1800s, many women organized to demand the vote. Elizabeth Cady Stanton was one of their leaders. Her words, presented on July 19, 1848, at a women's rights gathering known as the Seneca Falls Convention, were like those of Thomas Jefferson. But the small change expressed a big dream of equality that millions of women across America shared.

Another seventy-two years passed before Stanton's dream was fulfilled. In 1920, the Nineteenth Amendment to the U.S. Constitution was ratified, giving women the right to vote.

1852

FREDERICK DOUGLASS

What to the American slave is your Fourth of July?

I answer: a day that reveals to him,

more than all other days of the year,

the gross injustice and cruelty to which

he is the constant victim.

To him, your celebration is a sham; your boasted liberty,

an unholy license . . .

Frederick Douglass was an escaped slave living in Rochester, New York. A group of prominent citizens asked him to give a speech on the topic of Independence Day. Slavery was illegal in many northern states, so they assumed Douglass would speak about the freedoms he enjoyed in New York. But the people of Rochester were in for a surprise. Douglass had not forgotten the millions of black Americans who still lived as slaves across the South. His powerful words shocked and angered the crowd.

Throughout his life, Douglass used his abilities as a writer and a speaker to urge his fellow Americans to unite in the struggle for equal rights. Although the practice of slavery was abolished during Douglass's lifetime, legislation on equal rights would happen gradually over the next century.

SITTING BULL

*What treaty have the Sioux made with the white man
that we have broken? Not one.
What treaty have the white man ever made with us
that they have kept? Not one.
When I was a boy the Sioux owned the world;
the sun rose and set on their land;
they sent ten thousand men to battle.
Where are the warriors today?
Who slew them?
Where are our lands?
Who owns them?*

The source of this quote is unclear, but it is believed to be part of a speech that Sitting Bull delivered in about 1858.

Sitting Bull was a member of the Lakota Sioux. In 1870, the U.S. government forced his people to leave their homeland in the Black Hills of South Dakota. Sitting Bull tried to negotiate with the government to have the land returned. The U.S. government broke treaties and ignored protests from Native Americans. In response, Sitting Bull led his people in a long and violent struggle against the government.

Efforts on the part of the Sioux to regain the Black Hills continued long after Sitting Bull's death. In 1980, the Sioux were awarded $106 million in payment for the land. But they refused to accept money in exchange for their dream of returning to their home. They demanded the land instead. Laws that would have returned the Black Hills have twice been defeated in the U.S. Congress, but the Sioux continue the fight.

1863

ABRAHAM LINCOLN

All persons held as slaves within any state . . .
shall be . . . thenceforth and forever free.

After winning the 1860 U.S. presidential election, Abraham Lincoln dreamed of ridding the nation of slavery forever. The Civil War (1861–1865) between the Union and the Confederacy was raging during his term in office. Slavery was already abolished in most of the states of the Union. He wrote a document—called the Emancipation Proclamation—ordering that slaves in the rebellious Confederate states be freed, leaving slavery intact in some of the border states. Nonetheless, the proclamation was an important step in ending slavery. The final version of the Emancipation Proclamation was approved on January 1, 1863. The Confederacy did not recognize the authority of the government, so the proclamation was ignored and slavery continued in the Southern states. In May 1865, the Civil War ended, and the nation was reunited. The Emancipation Proclamation went into effect nearly three years after it was signed, when, on December 18, 1865, the Thirteenth Amendment to the Constitution was ratified. The practice of slavery was officially over. Within five years, the Fourteenth and Fifteenth amendments would be ratified, requiring all states to provide equal protection under the law to all people and making it illegal to deny a citizen the right to vote based on "race, color, or previous condition of servitude."

EMMA LAZARUS

Give me your tired, your poor,

Your huddled masses yearning to breathe free,

The wretched refuse of your teeming shore.

Send these, the homeless, tempest-tossed, to me,

I lift my lamp beside the golden door.

These are the last lines of a poem that is engraved on a plaque mounted on the Statue of Liberty. The poem, called "The New Colossus," was written by Emma Lazarus. Lazarus was not an immigrant, but she understood the challenges facing new arrivals to her nation, and she used her fame as a poet to work on behalf of immigrants.

In the late nineteenth and early twentieth centuries, the sight of the Statue of Liberty greeted immigrants entering the United States through the harbor of New York City. These courageous newcomers had left their cultures and most of their possessions behind to fulfill their dreams of freedom and opportunity.

FRANKLIN D. ROOSEVELT

I pledge you, I pledge myself, to a new deal

for the American people.

These words are from Franklin Delano Roosevelt's 1932 acceptance speech for the Democratic Party's nomination for president. As president during most of the Great Depression (1929–1942), Roosevelt strove to give Americans reason to hope for a better day. Along with his words of encouragement, he conceived the New Deal, a body of laws designed to hasten the economic recovery of a severely weakened nation.

Although he was born and raised in an extremely wealthy family, Roosevelt came to champion those most severely devastated by the Great Depression. After proposing higher taxes for the rich, Franklin Roosevelt saw his family expelled from the social club where they were members. But even after this rejection by those of his own economic class, Roosevelt refused to give in. He continued his fight to assure that all citizens were able to share in the American dream of freedom and prosperity.

FOR A NEW DEAL

FREE
CUP COFFEE & DOUGHNUTS
FOR THE UNEMPLOYED

FREE SOUP

1960

JOHN F. KENNEDY

Ask not what your country can do for you—
ask what you can do for your country.

This quote was part of President John F. Kennedy's inauguration address in January 1960. During his brief presidency (1961–1963), Kennedy inspired Americans to become more involved in their government. He created the Peace Corps, an organization dedicated to promoting world peace and friendship. Young men and women were sent to nations where trained workers were in short supply. Often working without electricity or running water in remote rural areas, they made a difference around the world.

Since its formation in 1961, more than 195,000 courageous Peace Corps volunteers have helped people in 139 countries fulfill their own dreams of a better tomorrow.

1962

RACHEL CARSON

*For the first time in the history of the world,
every human being is now subjected to contact
with dangerous chemicals,
from the moment of conception until death.*

Rachel Carson's book, *Silent Spring*, shocked Americans by its charges that chemical insecticides were poisoning their nation's water and farmlands. In her study, Carson discovered that traces of DDT, a widely used insecticide, were even present in the breast milk of nursing mothers. By making people aware of the perils of chemical pollution, the book also fostered the beginning of what would eventually become the environmental movement.

A committee appointed by President John F. Kennedy verified many of Carson's claims. In 1970, six years after Carson's death, the Environmental Protection Agency was formed, and two years after that, DDT was outlawed.

DR. MARTIN LUTHER KING JR.

I have a dream that one day

on the red hills of Georgia

sons of former slaves and the sons

of former slave owners will be able to sit down together

at the table of brotherhood.

I have a dream that my four little children

will one day live in a nation

where they will not be judged by the color of their skin

but by the content of their character.

Speaking from the steps of the Lincoln Memorial during the March on Washington on August 28, 1963, Martin Luther King Jr. scanned the crowd of more than a quarter million and delivered the above words.

In so doing, he informed and inspired Americans about what was truly happening in a nation that claimed to treat all people equally but was falling sadly short. The following year, major legislation was enacted in the form of the Civil Rights Act of 1964, making racial discrimination in schools, the workplace, and public places illegal.

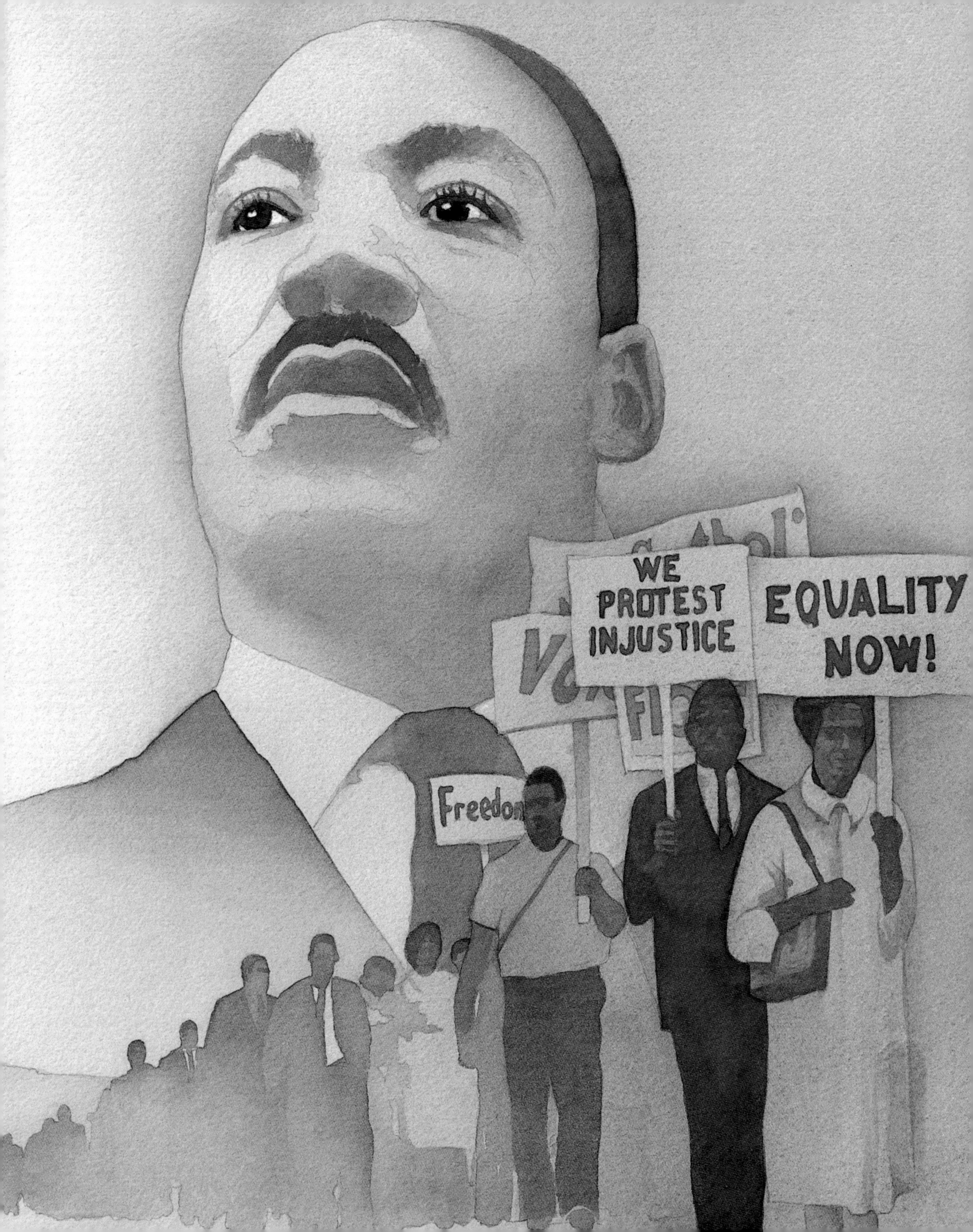
WE PROTEST INJUSTICE
EQUALITY NOW!

CESAR CHAVEZ

Across the San Joaquin valley, across California, across the entire nation, wherever there are injustices against men and women and children who work in the fields— there you will see our flags—with the black eagle with the white and red background, flying. Our movement is spreading like flames across a dry plain.

Cesar Estrada Chavez spoke the above words at a rally of the United Farm Workers of America, a union he helped create. Chavez was a farm laborer, an activist, and a union organizer. He spent his life fighting courageously in support of the rights of thousands of migrants who worked on farmlands that stretched from the apple orchards of upstate New York to the vineyards of California.

Borrowing from the nonviolent methods of Mohandas Gandhi and Dr. Martin Luther King Jr., Chavez rallied people around the world to boycott the grapes produced by growers who were mistreating their farmworkers. At one point, surveys showed that 17 million Americans were honoring the grape boycott. This eventually forced the growers of California to recognize the 1975 California Agricultural Labor Relations Act, which provided a legal framework for the union to represent all the nation's farmworkers in its negotiations for better wages, hours, and working conditions.

1990

ROSA PARKS

I would like to be known as a person who is concerned about freedom and equality and justice and prosperity for all people.

Many historians have written that the beginning of the civil rights movement took place on December 1, 1955. That was the day a black seamstress from Montgomery, Alabama, defied the law by refusing to give up her bus seat to a white passenger. After the incident, Rosa Parks was arrested and fined for violating a city ordinance. But her act of courage inspired a movement that hastened the end of racial segregation under U.S. law.

BARACK OBAMA

America is a land of big dreamers and big hopes.
It is this hope that has sustained us through revolution
and civil war, depression and world war,
a struggle for civil and social rights,
and the brink of nuclear crisis.
And it is because our dreamers dreamed
that we have emerged from each challenge more united,
more prosperous, and more admired than before.

These words were part of Barack Obama's commencement address at Knox College on June 4, 2005. They were delivered during a time of uncertainty, when Americans struggled to regain their sense of hope and optimism about the future.

Three years later, during his campaign that would result in his becoming the first African American U.S. president, Obama chose the word *hope* as his central message. Appearing in magazines, on posters, on television, and on the Internet, his bold message told Americans that change was possible, that big dreamers could once again make change happen. Working together, Americans could restore dreams of dignity and courage for themselves and their nation, giving birth to an era of renewed idealism, prosperity, and hope.

CHANGE
WE CAN BELIEVE IN

THOMAS JEFFERSON (1743–1826)

Born in Albemarle County, Virginia, Thomas Jefferson was elected U.S. president in November 1800. Known for his fine mind and many interests, Jefferson was an accomplished author, a philosopher, an architect, an inventor, a gardener, and an archaeologist, as well as being the founder of the University of Virginia.

At a gathering of forty-nine Nobel Prize winners in 1962, President Kennedy remarked that "this is the most remarkable collection of talent and of human knowledge that has ever been gathered together in the White House—with the possible exception of when Thomas Jefferson dined alone."

ELIZABETH CADY STANTON (1815–1902)

A native of Johnstown, New York, Elizabeth Cady Stanton was born into a politically active family. Her father was a distinguished judge and a state legislator. She was given an unusually solid education for a woman of the time. She put it to good use as a social activist who fought for the abolition of slavery and, later, as a leading member of the early women's movement. Along with Susan B. Anthony, she spent many years fighting for women's right to vote.

FREDERICK DOUGLASS (CA. 1818–1895)

Born on a Maryland plantation, Frederick Douglass managed to teach himself to read and write. At the age of twenty, he escaped to freedom in the North. There he began a new life as a public speaker, a writer, a political leader, and an adviser to President Lincoln. Douglass became well known for his speaking ability, as well as the many essays he published in the *North Star*, a newspaper he created. In addition to advocating for the end of slavery, he was also a strong supporter of women's rights.

SITTING BULL (CA. 1831–1890)

Widely respected for his bravery and insight, Sitting Bull, known by his people as Tatanka-Iyotanka, became head chief of the Lakota Nation in about 1868. He was willing to honor treaties between the U.S. government and Native Americans, but his true fame was as a warrior, defending his land when treaties were broken. In June 1876, his warriors killed the soldiers of General George Armstrong Custer, in a battle known as Custer's Last Stand.

ABRAHAM LINCOLN (1809–1865)

Born in a one-room log cabin near Hodgenville, Kentucky, Abraham Lincoln was the son of uneducated farmers. As a young boy, he taught himself to read, and his love of books would later become legendary. Walking across miles of wilderness, he visited neighbors on surrounding farms to borrow their books. Remarkable as it might seem, Abraham Lincoln's formal education consisted of just eighteen months of schooling.

He was elected as the sixteenth president of the United States in 1860 and reelected in 1864. While still serving as president in April 1865, Lincoln was assassinated by John Wilkes Booth.

EMMA LAZARUS (1849–1887)

Born and raised in New York City, Emma Lazarus was able to trace her ancestry back to America's early Jewish settlers. A literary prodigy, she privately published her first book of poetry when she was just seventeen. The poet Ralph Waldo Emerson was so impressed with her work that he became her mentor.

Lazarus was a major contributor to prestigious literary magazines throughout her life and received critical acclaim for her work. When she died at the age of thirty-eight, she left behind a much-admired literary legacy as well as a battle cry for immigrant rights in the form of her best known poem, "The New Colossus."

FRANKLIN DELANO ROOSEVELT (1882–1945)

Roosevelt was born in Hyde Park in the Hudson Valley of New York State. Both his parents were from wealthy families, and Roosevelt grew up in an atmosphere of privilege. While Franklin was attending Harvard University, his fifth cousin, Theodore Roosevelt, was elected president of the United States. He soon became young Franklin's role model and hero.

In 1921, he was stricken with poliomyelitis. He fought the disease courageously, but it left him in a wheelchair for the rest of his life. Roosevelt was elected governor of New York in 1928, and he ascended to the presidency four years later. He was reelected three times, the only president in U.S. history to serve more than two terms.

JOHN F. KENNEDY
(1917–1963)

On November 22, 1963, President John F. Kennedy was gunned down by an assassin's bullet in Dallas, Texas. He had been in office less than three years. The youngest person ever elected president, Kennedy was born in Brookline, Massachusetts, on May 29, 1917. The son of Joseph Kennedy (a prominent businessman and U.S. ambassador to Great Britain) and Rose Fitzgerald (the daughter of John Fitzgerald, mayor of Boston and three-term member of Congress), John F. Kennedy volunteered for service in the U.S. Navy and fought heroically during the Pacific campaign of World War II. He was later awarded the Purple Heart and the World War II Victory Medal. After the war, JFK entered politics, serving as congressman and senator from Massachusetts, before being elected president in 1960.

RACHEL CARSON
(1907–1964)

Rachel Louise Carson was born on a small family farm near Springdale, Pennsylvania. As a child, she spent many days exploring nearby ponds, meadows, and forests, and learning about nature from her mother. She began writing stories at the age of eight and, at eleven, had a story published.

As an adult, she became a prolific writer whose books about the ocean won many awards and made her a famous science writer. Focusing on the many ways in which people were destroying the natural environment, Rachel Carson became known as one of America's first environmentalists.

DR. MARTIN LUTHER KING JR.
(1929–1968)

Born in Atlanta, Georgia, Martin Luther King Jr. was the son of a Baptist minister. While attending Morehouse College, Martin decided that he would follow in his father's footsteps. After studying the works of Mohandas Gandhi, the great pacifist leader and philosopher from India, King became a believer in civil disobedience, a nonviolent means of effecting change through such things as boycotts, sit-ins, and nonpayment of taxes. As a leader of the civil rights movement, he devoted himself to a nationwide effort to grant equal rights to African Americans, who had been denied those rights. Dr. King organized hundreds of marches, sit-ins, and nonviolent demonstrations, leading the struggle for racial equality. An assassin cut short his life's work in 1968.

CESAR CHAVEZ
(1927–1993)

The son of Mexican American immigrants, Cesar Chavez was a migrant farmworker and activist who dedicated his life to the poor farm laborers of America. He personally experienced the terrible conditions workers endured in the fields. Chavez led a strike for better wages and working conditions and in 1965 staged a twenty-five-day hunger strike to attract attention to the workers' plight. His efforts eventually led to many improvements in the lives of farmworkers. His March 31 birthday has become Cesar Chavez Day, a holiday recognized in eight U.S. states. Many parks, schools, and libraries have since been renamed in his honor throughout the United States.

ROSA PARKS
(1913–2005)

Rosa Louise McCauley Parks was born in Tuskegee, Alabama. She was a civil rights activist whom representatives of the U.S. Congress would later call the Mother of the Modern Day Civil Rights Movement. Her single act of defiance started a yearlong boycott of the Montgomery bus system by blacks. This, in turn, attracted the interest of a little-known Atlanta, Georgia, clergyman named Martin Luther King Jr.

Parks continued to be a symbol of the civil rights movement, and her work earned a number of awards, including the Presidential Medal of Freedom and a Congressional Gold Medal. At her death, Parks was accorded an honor usually reserved for presidents. Her casket was placed in the rotunda of the U.S. Capitol Building for two days so that the people of America could express their gratitude for her courageous work.

BARACK OBAMA
(1961–   )

Barack Hussein Obama grew up in Hawaii and Indonesia. He worked his way through college, graduating from Columbia University in 1983. At Harvard Law School, he became the first African American to serve as editor of the *Harvard Law Review*. After graduation, he worked as a community organizer in Chicago, Illinois. He served as U.S. senator from Illinois from 2005 until 2008. In 2009, Obama became the forty-fourth president of the United States, the first African American to hold that office.

SOURCE NOTES

Page 2
Bernard K. Duffy and Richard
W. Leeman, *American Voices: An
Encyclopedia of Contemporary Orators*
(Santa Barbara, CA: Greenwood
Publishing Group, 2005), 242.

Page 4
David Armitage, *The Declaration of
Independence* (Cambridge, MA: Harvard
University Press, 2007), 25.

Page 6
Sabrina Crewe and Dale Anderson, *The
Seneca Falls Women's Rights Convention*
(New York: Gareth Stevens, 2005), 5.

Page 8
Howard Zinn, *A People's History of the
United States: 1492–present* (New York:
HarperCollins, 2004), 182.

Page 10
Wayne Moquin and Charles Van
Doren, eds., *Great Documents in
American Indian History* (New York:
Praeger, 1973), 262.

Page 12
Horace Greeley, *The American Conflict:
A History Part II* (Whitefish, MT:
Kessinger Publishing, 2005), 263.

Page 14
Zinn, 649.

Page 16
William Cahn, *A Pictorial History of
American Labor* (New York: Crown
Publishers, 1972), 250.

Page 18
Thurston Clarke, *Ask Not: The
Inauguration of John F. Kennedy and the
Speech That Changed America* (New
York: Macmillan, 2005), 4.

Page 20
Rachel Carson, *Silent Spring* (Boston:
Houghton Mifflin Harcourt, 2002), 15.

Page 22
Martin Luther King, Martin
Luther King Jr., and James Melvin
Washington, *A Testament of Hope: The
Essential Writings and Speeches of
Martin Luther King, Jr* (New York:
HarperCollins, 1991), 219.

Page 24
Carlos E. Cortés, *Three Perspectives on
Ethnicity–Blacks, Chicanos, and Native
Americans* (New York: Putnam, 1976), 381.

Page 26
Aasef Shafik, *Global Peace Lovers*
(Bloomington, IN: AuthorHouse,
2009), 233.

Page 28
Kate Burns, *Is the American Dream
a Myth?* (Farmington Hills, MI:
Greenhaven Press, 2006), 40.